On Watch
Lemon Sail the Sea

Gratitude to Grace Nichols and Roy Macfarlane for their inspiring words. And thanks to Cane Arrow Press for their continued support.

◊

'On Watching a Lemon Sail the Sea' was a prize-winner in the Welsh International Poetry Competition 2017. 'There, at the Bend of the River' is a video recording by New Welsh Review, Poetry Showcase, Fire and Water, on Vimeo in July 2015. 'Voyage in the Dark' was first published by Peepal Tree Press in the anthology, *Filigree*, in 2018. 'Lit by Fire' was commissioned and recorded at the North Foreland Lighthouse by the BBC for National Poetry Day 2016. 'Mrs Rosario's West Indian Siesta' was published in Poetry Wales, 2016. 'Coffee with Jean Rhys' is published in Wasafiri in 2019. Other poems have been published by The Caribbean Writer, Confluence magazine, Womanspeak, Thanet Writers and Interviewing the Caribbean, Derek Walcott Issue.

Maggie Harris was born in Guyana and has lived in the UK since 1971. A poet, short story writer and memoirist, awards for her work include The Guyana Prize for Literature and the Commonwealth Short Story Regional Prize. This is her sixth collection of poetry. www.maggieharris.co.uk

Also by Maggie Harris

Kiskadee Girl: Kingston University Press 2011
Canterbury Tales on a Cockcrow Morning: Cultured Llama 2012
Sixty Years of Loving: Cane Arrow 2014
In Margate By Lunchtime: Cultured Llama 2015
Writing on Water: Seren 2017

On Watching a Lemon Sail the Sea

Maggie Harris

Maggie Harris

Cane Arrow Press

First published 2019 by
Cane Arrow Press
PO Box 219
Royston
SG8 1AZ

Poems © Maggie Harris

British Library Cataloguing in Publication Data.
A catalogue record for this book is available from the British
Library

Cover photographs by Marcin Paluch

ISBN 978-0-9929388-3-3

CONTENTS

GUYANA

IRELAND

WALES

On Watching A Lemon Sail the Sea

1
and I'm singing 'You are my sunshine' thinking
of my childhood across the sea of incubation
go Honey go
you self-contained cargo ship you
with your sealed citrus juices and pitted panacea of seeds
braving the collision of tankers and illicit submarines

       they called me *scurvy*.   the lemonade
      my mother made was iced and sprinkled with
               Demerara
(of course)

and I'm wondering, did they grow you there, o lemon   mine
you
for your juices
a *lemon* plantation, not to be confused with
a *plantain* plantation even a banana just don't mention sugar
stack you in the gloom like hereto mentioned bananas
green and curtailed in their growing or even
those force-ripe mangoes with girls' names
nobody knows here and who leave their sweetness behind
bare-assed on the beaches
come
to the marketplace
comatose.

I do not remember lemons, but limes.
    M
  I   E
L   S.

Piled high in their abundance. Limes.
Acid green pyramids on market pavements
holding their secrets beneath their reptilian skins.

And there is my aunt, her arms thin as bamboo
gathering the fallen from the yard, sweeping
their dried leaves into the remembrance of herself
whilst the black maid slips slivers of lemon into a split
-bellied fish whose eyes glaze up at the sun.

'Gauguin, you can come in now; remember Martinique ...?
hue the *native* in all her harnessed beauty
the slack –jawed fish, browning blood
the textured landscape in shades of pawpaw and indigo.'

But, *liming* is what my lemon is doing now,
hey ho…
over the waves at Aberporth, there he blows.

2
I set you free
to take to the sea again
on a high tide, with breakers rushing the beach
like warriors.
They pummel the sand, scythe
a four-foot chasm into the mouth
of a lonely river
beat the rocks' submerged heads
batter the cliffs again
                    and again
                            and again.
The sea, beyond its charge, was waiting -
a winter morning sea, a Twelfth Night sea

12

tumultuous and moody

waiting.

A strange gift, you
a large, perfect lemon
fresh and sharp as the sun-bright
wind-cut winter's day. But I
unsure of your heritage
refused you.

3
Dear Voyager,
I cupped you
in my palm
desire urging my possession
how easy it would be – a lemon drizzle cake
a Martini iced, an accompaniment
to plaice or sole – and here I am playing with words
the resonance of belonging, of immortality –
but the devil played tricks with my mind
an injection of poison perhaps, a needle prick
into your pristine, nobbled skin – but we are running ahead here
thinking of cargo – you may simply have fallen from a Tesco
carrier bag whose owner, fearing a lonesome home-coming
went walking on these very sands contemplating - life.

But there you were anyway, settled on the sand like a crab
then comfortable in the palm
of my hand.

4

Finders are not necessarily keepers. Some
will do well to remember that. Vixens
circling misunderstood husbands in bars. Frag
ments from the fallen.
Oh but, how strong is the desire
to hold close, keep tight
smother your darling, your little nut-baby
in soft gloves, hard love, the kind that makes
you want to bite, bite! Rip flesh and bone. Swallow.
            I could have accepted
your sacrifice
that gift of yourself, thank the universe
for its' benevolence.
But the universe is not benevolent.
Stars are exploding missiles in a panther-black night.
Saturn doesn't give two fucks. It's chaos
out there.
But I guess you didn't have time
for star-gazing in your ocean-going lumbering
over the hey-ho waves. And if I had sunk my vampiric teeth
into the you of you, you would be no more
than a bitter taste, a withering lump of citrus
on my kitchen table. Far better to remember you
the obsidian walnut weight of you
and these questions you have gifted me
and that last sight of you
rolling away on the tide.

There At The Bend Of The River

There,
      at the bend of the river, I almost turned. I almost became
the   b r o k e n
        bough that floats, almost became a bride
          of the l a c y wake   almost borrowed the choir
          of incessant birds   almost forsook dry land
           for amniotic waters   almost didn't board
the taxi
        that led to the plane   that led to the city of deceit and
promise
      that would neverthe less
    enrich me with its tales and offer me lovers
to distract me.
          I almost   would not have born
e   these children who make their mark like   r
                                   a
                                   i
                                     n
        like SonG   b
          birds &   o
            bees   w
                                s
        like batons passing the   trail
      messages on their fingers like d u s t. There, at the bend
of the river,
words would not have   a l i g h t e d
  like a passenger
    on these still trembling chords   of my throat.

Driving Through Happy Valley

Driving through Happy Valley in a cherry-red Nissan
the cedars are whispering
a coniferous cathedral rising from the mountain, falling
from the slopes

Sheep feather the valley below
the body of a badger roughs the smooth road
centuries of heartbeats

        clavicles and mandibles, pterodactyl claws
        a compost of vixens, blooded and matted
        and slate: dull, calm, black slate.

Memory is cloven-hoofed, bristles of hair
boar-slow, lumbering through forests
lured by a scent of smoke
fairytale woodland

and my fingernails grip and scratch
back and back onto slate
break sticks of chalk
in a Guyanese school-room.

Cedars lived in poems then
fat-tongued and Lebanese, unrequited, unknown
a thicket of language picked and hacked
with the rough slash of cutlasses
singing of raid and conquest
Pict and Celt, Slave and shackles.

Now only caravans glint
through a birch's antlered brace
against a wild vertiginous hill
a blinding flash of sunlight sharp
as blades.

Not Home

Only by familiarity can I call this place Home
only by the world prowling its perimeters like a wolf
only by gratitude to the campervan, to so many of us caught
out, mid-life
burning bridges, upping sticks, heading for the hills with too
late, hippie hope.

No children were bred here; no school runs inviting intimacy
no anxious faces grouped at the gate like nuns.
Where this river runs, it runs unfettered by stones my child
might have thrown.
That cemetery above does not contain *our* ancestral bones.

We are still strangers in this mist. This chapel does not know me
does not care about hallelujahs from alien lands
or impoverished visitors bringing dust on their shoes from the
south.

I do not want to love you, even though your beauty flings itself
in my face
like that very first time: the montbretia like a whore in the
daytime
brazen, naked arms of gold.

My heart was already taken: that board house my father
wanders
under a twilight of stars
the semi on a southern coast, walled with the sound of growing
limbs
the palms settled there, like a sigh.

And even as I try, my hands in the soil seeding
transplanting the unloved heads of so many nameless ones
my heart is cold, I dare not love you.

Blackbird

He hops close to me today
his morning song broken
by the rumble of diggers
mowers, hedge-cutters
the two-octave whine of the strimmer
decapitating summer's wild children
the febrile limbs of toadflax, the paper wings of moths.

A tractor labours itself up the hill
past the digger's drill and dredge, shovels
whole clods of earth into its hungry mouth.

Imagine drones, jet fighters screaming
the implosion of tarmac
strips of bodies falling like ribbons.

He raises his head from the soil
looks at me. We wait
for things to settle
right themselves.

Portmeirion Birds

These birds in the cabinet now, our conversations have only just
begun
they tell me their names through the glass - scarlet tanagers
and orioles, bluebirds and chickadees, bullfinches, hoopoes,
egrets.
In return I sing to them of kiskadees and sandpipers, flamingos
potoos and swifts.
One day soon they will set me free, and their songs
anoint my tongue.

Stealing Stones

Stealing a stone from Abaraeron
guilt riding her Catholic shoulders, a demon
dressed in denim, anglicised.
She pauses at chapels, wondering
if Reason was yet another myth, wise men
and angry feminists swaying her mind
just like all those priests and nuns
with their Latin prayers and American tongues
had imprisoned her mother's calcified soul.

Here, in this new place, it is only the weight of stones
soothed by the bitter Atlantic
that lends some gravity
to the lightness of her steps on the gravel
her weightless gaze.

Garden Centre, Moylegrove

The curry plant is happy here, under cover
away from cold winds
the sea's rage.
His scent urges the rub between thumbs and fingers,
noses draw his otherness into themselves.
It's a cultural gathering: coriander and chillies
ginger, fennel, rosemary.
At night-time the air is filled with discourse
dialects jump like fireflies between the ginger and the canna
complaints about the draft, who was born of original seed.
Journeys are shared, passages of plastic and pearlite
the inconstant humidity, the brittle nature of neighbours.
But beneath the chorus, the fear of the open door.
When one by one they go, lifted
into wire baskets, bound for yet another
migration
their goodbyes are a heavy silence
in the tremble
of their filigreed leaves, good luck wishes
transmigrating over the compost bin
the till, and out into the Cardigan air.

At Ceibwr Bay

gathering on the bridge
sisters, daughters, grand-children
one by one and two by two
smiling into the sea

legs swing into empty space
over Nant Ceibwr, a river
restless to be free
rushing beneath these solid slabs of stone

lifted here, one imagines
by crane on a tractor
rolling along the cliff road on a fine day
wheels on tarmac, once clay
once horses and drays, lime, kilns
a ship with sails, anchored
in the bay

black cliffs
jack-knife into the Irish sea
sharp, primeval
slice the horizon, shadow
water swirling into coves
sweeping scalloped stones

river running, restless
tumbling
intent on displacing kayaks
and lone walkers dropping
from the coast path
photographers

perching on baptismal stones
family groups smiling into the unknown
history of ports
and anchors
before road, before rail
before us

but we are Caribbean
we know about discovery
are used to fixing ourselves
into the frame.

Let's walk to the Witches' Cauldron

Two steps on the path and I'm losing the will
    Let's walk to the Witches' Cauldron
Forgetting this morning those brave words falling
    Let's walk to the Witches' Cauldron
Safe in bed with brass backbone
    Let's walk to the Witches' Cauldron
The fear of vertigo rising
The hungry sea waiting
for my crushed bones on the rocks
    Let's walk to the Witches' Cauldron[1]

Beauty rears like beasts, these staggered rocks
the wind's cracked laughter, the abyss
the sky a chapel of pterodactyls
and small me, little me
in wooden shoes with leaden heels
heart louder than the corps of seagulls
wheeling, dipping, sneering like those girls
so long ago, more beautiful, more clever
their sporty limbs like shotguns
mine like hockey sticks
whilst I held the banner, passed the cup.

But.
Turn back now, I will never face a cliff again
never follow the longing
never erase the memory of the skinny girl at the back of the field

---

[1] The Witches' Cauldron is an inlet, a place of natural beauty in West
Wales, only accessible by a perilous coast path, or by kayak

one foot in front of the other, one hand on every blade of grass
both eyes on the track.
Don't. Look. Down.
Breathe   see the flat gravelled path   the froth of September
gorse
the dog nosing.   Listen   to the sing of the wind   a kestrel
dipping
the sudden opening of your chest like bellows
pumping your unpredictable heart.
The sea   *that* sea   that wavering noonday   catch-my-eye sea
just carrying on his business
his normal everyday business
tied by the moon and the tides   I am the last thing on his
mind.

And suddenly
I am as light as that curlew there
riding on the wind
    lift each leg up and around
earth
stone
step
and there

falling away like a heartbeat
into the song-sway of a gull's wing
one hundred soars below
  the Witches' Cauldron
twinkling in a setting of diamonds and light
sapphire blue   cerulean blue
embraced by causeway and stepping stones
and miniature kayaks with miniature men
dropped like a gift from the heavens

and from the earth a song comes
from the cliffs a chorus
from the sea the dolphins
from the path a causeway
thinning into infinity, singing
I've put a spell on you
I've put a spell on you.

On Constitution Hill

A golden boy, weather-kissed
smile open like the land/sea sweep
above Aberystwyth, on Constitution Hill.
Mercurial limbs in summer shorts
angled against the wind.
Labrador bounding
ears back, nose to ground.

Rusting cargo ships, my sister and me
salted to the timbers, schoonered by blood and bone
weakened Achilles' heels; our silver-haired men
with crampons and binoculars
impaling sea and sky.

Words whip between us like kites,
joy spills from the lips of the golden boy
travelling 'this stunning country',
Beast, his campervan, waiting
in some parking space below.

We want to pin him to the mast,
remembering easy conquests
in smoky bars and nightclubs
just yesterday, just last week.

We giggle like schoolgirls
swallow his words, drink his youth
wave him farewell with the arid taste of truth.

Welsh Poppies

My garden is singing with poppies
Welsh, yellow golden orioles
their hearts pin-pricked with summer.
Come the slightest breeze they dance
their petals paper-thin, faces bold to the sun.
Menace has no place here
evil does not lurk in the stone-packed earth
nor hide behind the ferns. The sun is shining
clear through their leaves, they are too diaphanous for
shadows.
Tragedy's dark burgundy weight
does not belong.

No-one has selected these for remembrance or peace,
so I will; I select them for the freedom to dance at will
they can sing as loud as they bloody well like
in whatever language they choose
for even when they die, their maracas seeds
will rumba and rattle an anthem loud to Kingdom Come.
Amen.

Slug Woman

She goes out into the night, in breastplate of nylon
in shoes that will withstand the damp
cushion the gravel, make little sound.

From a window she might be a firefly
pin-points of indeterminate light
flickering behind the hedgerow
alighting on flowerpots
rising to canes where sweet peas climb
to baskets which swing
with hosannas of lobelia
hallelujahs of geraniums
the come-on-down of asters

She's carrying weapons
both legal and not
in saucepans and bottles
like tridents

swoops like a policeman on cliff-top car parks
startling lovers by torch

Sometimes, sorrow comes
a moist body curling
like a foetus
in her palm

but one by one she drops them
refusing to forget

the seedlings

their passage
from packet to womb
the lift of their breathless pin-drop heads
breaking to look at the dawn
the threads of their roots
their fragile, troubled spirits
like eels on land

and she is their only saviour
their lady of the night
gathering her shadow like a ball-gown
adjusting its trail on the lawn
where the night like a lover waits
to pluck death from her hand.

After Paradise

For those who know the daily stings, the murdering, the
screaming hills, relentless ants a- armying
The hammock slung between the trees, a bed of hessian
unkempt, a slice of clear blue sky.
Rubber, copra, cancer cures a secret still, falling, dropping, dust
to dust beneath the chainsaw's kill.
There's no Columbus here.

In paradise the gardener's hands scythe furze and flesh and
thorns, her head is full of folk songs
Heads of corn like Aztec kings, the Sun God high, the peasants'
hearts a sacrifice to birthing
Her cotton skirt, a thread, a snag, on brambles' bleeding
blackened blood
The trail of slime her nightly vigil, bowls of ale, baptismal fonts
for slugs and snails
Their bodies curled like foetuses, slung to compost heaven.
There are no fireflies here.

The moon holds fast her moodied face, selects the fickle clouds
to skim the light she offers
Offers up her chambered heart, her sectioned heart, her Chelsea
Gardens' arteries
Their walls of water, walls of stone, the perfect cloistered rose
Divine, divide, deduce, design, the sculptured lawns like
drawing rooms
Compact the mass of locust, lust, vertebrae and bones in their
moonless catacombs

With muddied boots, with hoe and rake, smooth the rape of
history

Tidy all the jagged edges, fallen leaves, the budding heads of
un-named weeds
Pile them on the compost heap, watch them burn, then leave.

Coffee With Jean Rhys

We recognise each other by our voices, laminated English on
back-home patois
hot-house force-ripe women seeking glasshouses and men to
stoke the belly fire.
You eye me warily, used to mis-interpretation, twisted words,
lies.
Selfish, I want to ask about Madox Ford, none of *my* lovers were
literary men
and now that youth is gone ...
Your blue eyes stare out the window, glance at me briefly over
the steam.
Wales lies between us like a dream.
I'm thinking about tales; the public you, the private you,
you at Cheriton Fitzpaine
pissed as a fart on champagne.
I wish I could have been there. I want to be pissed too,
to accept an honorary doctorate with tipsy hands, share the
synchronicity
of us both retiring to cold countries away from the imaginary
centre.
But when I look in the window there is no reflection, only a
stifled air
and the cut-glass accents of critics
ordering tea.

ENGLAND

Peeling the Potatoes

That day I first peeled a potato
wanting to be grateful
knowing nothing of Raleigh apart from my bike back home
and the tale of him laying down his cloak for his queen.
I filled the big pot with water
scraping the skins with un-accustomed hands.
Beyond the frosty window London loomed
Harrow-on-the-Hill, rooftops, pigeons
double-decker buses.
They were late home from Guildford
having eaten, angry at the waste
from this teenager dropped into their living-room
kipping on their couch
suitcases still labelled Guyana
a country they knew nothing about
apart from the fact they grew sugar there,
and rice.

Lit By Fire[2]

When the parakeets sing I listen;
they parlay a riotous sound,
like children braving the boundless waves
as loud as conch and flute and drum
from Norse and Viking men and
others since who brave this surging sea
for safety or possession, or roam
all shores and oceans; what restless souls
you human beings are!

They are the sound, I am the light.

Whoever lit a beacon first did so in my name
and here I stand: this clifftop mine;
manned or not it is *I* who shine.

There are cabbages now, around my feet
as I look out over Joss Bay where surfers ride
and shipwrecks sleep.
There are horses too, and sometimes sheep
golfers swing, and dogs race up the steep concrete
to furrow of earth and chalk complete
with the memory of plough and timber, lath and plaster
the tower built, the fire lit, the wind's teeth, the sea's bite
gnashing on a body of souls.

Then brick, stone, flint, coal. Re-building the bones of the *I*
that I am, trusted with the safety of every fleet

---

[2] North Foreland Lighthouse, Broadstairs

from London to Atlantic Shores
oak-bottomed buttressed galleons
Indiamen, cavalry, sailor and fisherman
Princesses, Kings, Orangemen, slaves,
all watching for my guiding light through
savage rocks and treacherous Goodwins
waiting still for vessels now within my keep -
tankers, pleasure boats, ferries
sailing past that *other* farm
where soldiers clad in sails of white
and wings of steel, are armoured to the Channel's floor
harnessing the wind.

Between us urgent messages
run with the rhythm of thundering hooves
over oystered bones and rusted gold;
ghosts rush up my spiral stairs
their bodies damp and cold -
The *Albion*, 1849. The *Northern Belle* and *Victory*, 1857.
The *Herald of Free Enterprise*, 1987...

Now golf balls spin and babies grin
tractors chew the Norsemen's lute
a feather from a black-backed gull
dances in the aerial light
and small laughs break from the convent girls
in their walk down to the shore.
I settle them all in my crown of light
to burn like stars and blaze
their right to life and journeys
free and wild for all eternity.

Crossing the Lawn

She hesitates to cross the lawn, her mother-in-law is holding out
a thorn
a David Austen rose impaled, perfume clings to her like burrs.
It will take a generation to propagate an interest, to bring forth
her familiar
a seedling bursting forth with such an utterance, the morning
wept.
It would take a generation, transmigration codes like microchips
the brambles' spite, jiggers in the mind, the heads of cane like
penises.
Of tidy lawns and borders edged, of Latin names and colour
schemes
of seasons and the quality of soil, she has not yet discovered.
Crossing the lawn, she is still a cart borne down in mud
her spirits and her body crushed, the sugar spilt like blood.

Drowning

In the drying sweat of our love you tell me how
not once, but twice, you nearly drowned
playing boyhood games in the Wensum.
And for a moment you are back there,
breathing not air, but water, and there are reeds
stroking your face, not my hair, and our daughter,
our lovely daughter, dancing in that photograph
there above the mirror, would never have been.

A Lake Hotel, Keswick

Old lovers, returning to a hotel where memory trapped them
within Scandinavian walls, white sheets imprinted with their
shape
the shower of glass, her body opening to his against the tiles.
The car pulling in to the drive some twenty years later
recollection like the indeterminate sky over Cat Bells
time a cocoon, two decades through which a world corrupted
by 9/11 and smart phones remembers things differently.
This is where they sat, ate, but *this* has changed. These.
The lake was not *that* close.
Outside the new conservatory, blue tits crowd the feeder
sheep wander the lawn. Saplings have become trees,
etch the waterline.
The tea when it comes, is a sacrament shouldered by
priestesses in black, the ritual unchanged,
silver on china, infusion, stir, pour;
sugar evaporating like steam.

Thanking Mr Walcott

The man I live with is full with the love of birds
although he no longer considers me one
I have advised him to read Jean Rhys
The Wide Sargasso Sea
and acquaint himself with Mr Rochester
who almost lost himself in the love
of a Caribbean woman. We are a breed apart
and sometimes people can't take too much of us.
Like curry.
It's something seeing a young bird trilling in the wild.
Quite another to bring it inside, give it a home
in the front room. Another thing again to turn your house
into a hide, watch the blue tits and magpies vie for the
titbits outside, pin them down with your binoculars and the desire
to be able to fly. The thing about flying is
you need wings, and to grow them you need
to become another creature entirely.
That's when the whole business gets crazy.
At least we have Mr Walcott, who has compared us
to swifts, we sleep on the wing, our sharp shadows
a congregation of stars.

Fells

You encircle me like eagles
　　　　　large wings beating slowly

in the undulation of light
and shadow
gorse-green, gold, Chilean chocolate
snow-crested, palette-thick.
Sometimes the wolves within you run,
changing your shape into hunchback or vixen
racing beneath the wind-sharp clouds
that can turn like a twist
into laundry.
And only when I reach the lake, stare
at you immersed in water
are you temporarily still, pausing
as one does, for a photograph.

Heron

Sickle-shape silhouette on black-water tarn
ghost-white, statue-still
against muddied trees
reed-thin legs submerged
within pond-weed and lilies

He is a conduit between earth and sky
alert to the procession
of walkers, dogs, sticks, cameras;
following their passage
with panoramic eyes

A dancer, a diviner
an arabesque on the water
scooping small creatures
from their universe of mud

he himself
ready at any moment
to rise like smoke
into the air

Wishbones

She boards the bus, becoming
in the moment before she scans her pass
the young Liz Taylor, violet eyes, pearl-white smile
at the bus driver who waves her in dismissively

heads for her usual seat, three rows back
watches the girl with the twins
their faces ringed with chocolate

The bus leaves the village, rides
through fields of rape.
If she squints she could see cane
see herself and her brother sneak
through the fields in Demerara
the coolie cutters slicing segments
with blooded cutlasses, offering them
to the two high-colour children who later
will squat on the back-step sucking them dry
distilling juice from fibre, tossing
the husks like marbles and wishbones.

In Tesco she pushes the trolley, bypasses
the salads and nuts, crisps and steaks
reaches for potatoes and mangoes, wondering
what could replace the longing.

On the ride home, the pain beats down
and she wonders where her baby teeth
lie buried, little tombstones
in that earth better known now, for sugar than gold
and she readies herself for that unfamiliar face

that will greet her in the hall mirror
when she takes out her plate
reaches for the soup bowl.

Collection

A world away now, those Bible stories...

        Sunday afternoons after Church
everything quiet quiet. No radio playing
    no sweeties allowed, no comic books, no outside,
everything of the earth laid to rest.

The morning mass stilled
the march of mantillas
the starch of white shirts
the rustle of organdie
the sheen of patent shoes.

Silently down the aisle the verger slid
the brass bowl, passed along the pews
for offerings
coins of the poor, dollars of the rich
whilst from the pulpit the sermon
cut like a siren: a Jesus driving the money
lenders from the temple.

Sundays now, roads nose to tail
from Sainsbury to B & Q
checkouts ring incessantly, loud as bells.

I can see my grandfather now, condemning us all to hell.

Canary Girls, 1915, 2015

1915
The baby's skin is yellow.
like her mother's. Together their screams
travel back-to-back yards, grey washing
green fields, urban grasses
the munitions factory where
yellow women sing, pack TNT into flasks
penile shapes dreaming of puncturing another earth
exploding like the sun.

2015
Tonight Number 8 man call her Satellite
Ambassador of Nations
his head fall on her shoulder and cry
Number 9 tell her she do good and soon
will be her own apartment with balcony
where they can have drink and watch the stars

what she knows about stars is what she sees when she falls
explosion in her head *Pow!* and other girls
remembering Grandfathers taking singing birds
below ground and others
pointing bears and hunting dogs in night skies above homes
in other continents deep with mountains
before wolves come
before trucks and boats and rooms
with no windows no night or day and men
breaking them in like horses with McDonalds breath
and fucking.
Car windows glide.
Headlamps and hubcaps torch the pavement

on bears and foxes, wolves, dustbins.

Darkness drops no stars, but sometimes
high up on balconies, canaries sing.

Here's Looking at you, Kid

Here's looking at you, Kid
a drink to you now you've gone
against a backdrop of hospital beds and white sheets.
That silhouette I quickly replace, instating
that one of you, head back laughing
a cigarette between your fingers and lips
Bogart in *Casablanca*.
Snap again: a horseman riding across Pinar del Rio
tobacco farmer in a battered Panama
red earth, dog following, etched against the sunset.
And snap again: the Marlborough ad, cool
American hero, blue jeans, blue eyes weathered.

Here's looking at you, Kid.
Would you have done it any different?
Living the full life in a seaside town, beset by images
of manliness, your hardening hands?
No, I don't believe so; that curl of smoke unfurling
in a blue haze, belonged to pubs, music, laughter
the Public Bar, Stella beer mats
the camaraderie of young men; girls in laddered
tights and low-cut tops turning on a bar-stool
for a light

and old men: backing into corners with a pint
rheumy eyes filming re-runs of *The Great Escape*.
Here's looking at you, Kid
I'll play it again, and again.

Daphne Laments her Coming to Age

We are no longer friends, my body and I.
We no longer laugh together or blush at illicit plans
for Saturday night or Sunday morning.
We are no longer our fisherwoman's mouth
spitting out communion wafers, or our un-anointed skin
lovers had slid so eagerly, following
the salted passages of their tongues.

Mercy then to angled limbs
and crumpled frocks like cassocks on the sandblast floor
damn all the devils waiting with their fiery forks.

We are no longer friends, my body and I.
We are no longer honouring the High Street
or palm-lined beaches with our dimpled butt
rippling in satin recklessness. No.
We eye our Self warily, circling our focus like wagon trains
haul up Apache leggings to cover the belly
the babies had swum in pre-Caesarean abandon.
We're grateful for working knees and feet that toodle–oo
down midnight stairs in search of the loo
for the ability to manage a Salsa, and the feat
of toenail cutting.

Only with the descent of night do we communicate again
our fingers becoming the light switch
someone had turned off sometime around the millennium.

It's party time then, that girl coming out from backstage
her skin so fucking alive and glowing
shock after shock of e-lectricity

lifting her off her backside
like motorbikes boarding the promenade
on a Bank Holiday, the sun blinding the crinkling
of her leatherette skin.

Women Weaving

Of need or the simple desire to make things
the women sit and spin.
Eternity, whirling,
drops into conversations where the tongue
halted in its realm of language
forces its way through clay and wool
the threaded knot of fingers

through the sensuous, through patterns
embossed in cochineal, stabbed by quills
skein of silk, blood of herringbone
labyrinthine oscillation of thumbs.

Language independent of words, dependent
only on air travelling through lungs
and the reeling skein by skein of fisherwomen's fingers
negotiating the landscape of foreign things.

Voyage in the dark
For Hilary

We swim towards each other in the dark.
An oily dark, buoyed by tentacles of memory
that brush past our ears like feathers. Inconstant
syllables linger, phrases regroup and reform;
your turquoise earrings swing in their film
of silver against your cheek.

Your eyes float towards me in the gloom.
Elizabeth Taylor eyes, they once danced with mirth
and innuendo, head tipped back for another glug
of wine, poetry tossed with pancakes
and metaphors mixed as salads.

You can no longer make tea. Your kitchen
is a place of unfamiliar things you wander
with lost hands. We are marooned here.
Seamus Heaney is still in the shed. Plath
and Hughes drop in, revitalise
our meetings as they always do, shine
a light on our constant tussle with ideas and form.
Sometimes Walcott returns, like the *Wide Sargasso Sea,
Sugar and Slate, 'that lovely Charlotte'*, me,
those you welcomed with open palms.
I stroke the vein-blue thin of your hands,
From far away the clock booms
another hour.

On Not Being Frida Kahlo

In this tale the children have hammered their way out of her
ribcage
like woodpeckers; they are ruthless and persistent
shredding through tissue and bone until they scatter the residue
into filaments of neon.

Husbands pace back and forth smoking cigars
under narrowed eyes in the glare of the sun, their sure feet
                 and solid bodies planted like corn.

When the fledglings land they scream the moistness of their
feathers
dry in one long bloody scream that forces each broken rib to
fuse
with the terror of survival, and as if to soften her resistance
they become so beautiful, so vulnerable, she gathers them up
and settles them in the crevices of her armpits
and the cracks of her limbs, like bromeliads
in the shade of their fathers' light.

Black, she dances
Turner Contemporary, Margate

The tutu spins
in the gallery
suspended from the ceiling
a crow with weather-battened feathers
a black star erupting. Outside
the sea rushes the window
heaving with history and intention.
Inside her the spirit
of Arachne, an Odile
dismissed, given the heave-ho by some Athena,
remains on stage defiant
transformed
into a dervish
permanently
whirling
the birth
of Anansi.

On acquiring a Banana from Eden

Banana, I crown you King of the Backyard,
Chief amongst the dahlias and alliums, the sweet peas.
Yours was a frayed welcome to this broken earth with its shards
of glass
and splintered shed where un-named weeds proliferated,
strangled earthworm, ivy, fencing.
I had wrenched you from Eden through my mercantile grasp
my romantic predilection for anything remotely tropical
driving you from Cornwall to Kent in a beat-up motor-home;
yet another migration of longing.
All summer you grew glossy and elegant, each few days
another leaf unfolding, shaped like an ixwa, gathering irises
and petunias at your feet whilst the tree fern loitered in the
shade.

And then the North Wind whipped in over the English Channel,
snapping your new bananalings into a ragtail of flumes
and feathers whilst you stood stem-naked, war-torn

reminding me of Frida;
not surprising as I'd just seen her in the V&A
scarred and beautiful, her corsets of leather and steel
her built-up shoe a vessel of survival.

Your resistance is as solid;
her Mexican skirts planted her in the earth like a windmill
an embroidered Dalek gliding through her garden with Diego,
her head crowned with blooms.

I will cosset you as winter approaches
wrap you up in the love that migrants need to acclimatise

look forward to the day when your head uncurls from the froth of
fleece and I can look through the kitchen window
and say Yes, Glory Be.

—

Harvey the Hemingway Cat

Wild thing, how could I love you and leave you
when at five weeks, a strayling, a home-seeker, you clutched at
my sweater
with claws that could not yet retract

fit like a mitten into the cup of my palm and travelled wide-
eyed
from Kent to Somerset to Wales, where you lived within stone
and woodland
leapt with joy at butterflies, hid in the rose arch ready to strike

You grew used to trees and open fields
brought us gifts of rats and voles and little Jenny wren
came walking with us along the track, running up trees and
pouncing
on the dog's back

We listened out for your dash through the cat-flap
your six-toed thump down the stairs
where you soon transformed from wild cat into lap cat
the stretch on your back belly-up cat
the seeking the sun by the door cat
the ready to leap for a Dreamie cat and even a lick of red wine

But we couldn't live there any longer and a town life is not for
you
not this postage stamp garden and busy roads
too urban for you my little six toed darling my three years of
pleasure and joy

For to love is to let go and now, you're a Somerset cat

with all the love you could wish for and fields all rich for the
picking
with rabbits and squirrels and birds

and when you walk past when I visit
tail up on your way out the door, I'm the only one bothered
not you, and that's exactly how it should be.

GUYANA

Alphabet Shanty

To that first Miss who brought me letters
etched on slate   the singing gate
white chalk on black   my skin, her skin
the *A* becoming *apples*
        the sun outside a singing-so
        a-singing so
        the women off to market o to market o
four years old   my fingers are bananas
snap the stick of chalk
        my tears are all a-running so
        a-running so
        i want to run the open door

the *aforapple* on the line
a again and *a* again
half a teacup   half a moon
a quarter of a petal
        the boy next door a-crying so
        a-crying so
but teacher's voice a-whispering
rub out chile and try again
have a go another go   another go

then through the window comes the breeze
i bite my lip to concentrate
the squeak of chalk on powdered slate
her hand on mine   the rise the fall
the slant the curl the loop the crawl
            and then i am a-sailing so!
            the chalk become my tiller o
            on slate of ocean sailing so

her breath the breeze
my arm the sail
and over the waves we go we go
over the waves we go!

After hearing (Wordsworth's) Daffodils, the Star-Apple decided to Sing

Their chants fly out the school-room window, rise like a choir of mosquitoes,
fleet and reed-like through the heavy heat. Children.
In their confusion they patter those words learnt by heart;
by noon they will swivel out into the yard and cluster beneath me
with their slingshots and gum, their Creole tongues
relinquished from English.
The words they chant are a mystery to me.
I know not what is a daffodil.
I know not what is a host.
The only hosts here are parasites that burrow and eat us all from the inside out
or haunt these churches left and right with their bread and wine and Holy Ghosts
prayer flags and night-time drums summoning ancestors
across the ocean floor.
I know not what is Spring; there are no seasons here but rain or shine
my leaves are dry and crisp, I long for rain but when it comes
the Goddess Rainstorm cries unceasingly, whole waterfalls of loss
as symmetrical as sugar-cane
ploughing a landscape of blood and bone.
But when these children gather, raise their eyes to heaven
through my diamante leaves, pluck my fruit and suck as if their life depended on it,
this is the spring I can offer – the future - and whatever it brings.

The Tales My Mother Told Me

...   didn't come from books
I can't remember her turning a page by the side of our beds
with the unpredictable electric light flickering overhead.
                Her stories were not bedtime stories but tales
of childbirth, deathbeds, prophesy, orphans
black and white, runaways, child-brides and Gods,
in all their transformations.
The sound of her voice in our home-rhythms
story-teller, life-giver, bringing the world
to the rocking chair with her warm
breath and pauses, a sip of water, laughter, tears,
memory unfolding with an *oh yes, that was it* ...

The monsters were the other side of the jalousies,
Spite and Envy, Greed and Cruel,
jumbies and old higues, bacoo and churile
the walking dead who sat down beside you
bringing their scents of lily of the valley, mud and rum.

When we crossed the water
they came too
made their home in the medicine cupboard
and under the floorboards, waiting
to carry on the conversations
still churning, like millstones
in our heads.

After Paradise, 2

Coming from paradise I'm aware of its' sting, of sand-flies at
dusk
their peppered kisses, the mosquitoes' lunatic singing.
They compete with my lover's bites on the porch, anointing my
neck
in the pin-prick light of the fireflies' flight.
The floor of the kitchen is alive with roaches: their corpuscular
bodies scramble over the can of Flit, run the lino, circle the
mangle.

None of them care that my lover is forcing my thighs apart
on greenheart wood sighing with the recollection of rain
or of Raleigh's insectile steps through virgin soil
or of woodants making dust of millennia of memory
in the force of his every thrust.
These brochures now, their promises
of palm trees and mojitos
harbouring these secret lies
as thin
as the paper
the ink
bleeds
on.

White

When the Governor-General died they wore white.
White, they said, to celebrate his life, not mourn it.
The white was blinding.
Polyester and linen drooped in the heat like washing.
Cotton and seersucker knew better, they were used
To starch and heat, parodied the stiff upper lips
Through the trumpets of lilies arrayed on the gun-carriage.
The women's gloves were star-shaped banners
Stiffly dismissing tears that threatened to spoil things.

Later his wife collapsed into the arms of black maids
Her eyes red-rimmed as the sorrel they brought her
The blood pumping around her stateless heart
Like the chicken they sacrificed in the yard
Drop by bloody drop.

Caribbean Soup, 1959

When the radio start playing Elvis, Mavis pounding the foo-foo
her arms powdered with flour from the fry fish and the bakes
dancing in the oil, sizzling in the karahi puff up like blowfish.
Yellow plantains waiting, vex to be a side dish
not the main where Mavis now tossing in the big guys
eddo and cassava, wild thyme and pimento
left hand sprinkling, right hand pounding, mouth
miming the words to *Wooden Heart.*
Behind her, the washing machine throttle charging up
ready for his ricketics, shaking the floor-boards
rattling the cooler, jangling the coffee and the Red Rose tea
to samba, jerk up the table where Mavis now balling up the foo-
foo
ready to drop them one by one in the soup-come-to-boil
remembering the loving-up last Saturday, how the man spoil
she, call she 'sweetmeat', refusing to discuss his wife
and wondering why now they have to play that stupid song
just when she getting the seasoning just right?

Mrs Rosario's West Indian Siesta

The rain pelting down don't make nothing better
Mrs Rosario in her balloon of heat on the daybed
tossing and turning
she can't get no sleep with the God-spite rain
bladdering down on the repair roof
pissing himself with anti-paradise
parasitical venom.
She following his progress in the Straits
capsizing the pirogue down past all the shipwrecks
then back to his antics in the over-flowing gutter
fish-gut voices vociferous in his wake.

Mrs Rosario trying to catch some shut-eye
dreaming up fanciful English country lanes
and tidy rain, fields with sheep jumping stiles
and that picture with her Granny dress smart
outside a place call Dorset, roses and thatch.
Shame they dint stay there save theyself
all this trouble; look her own skin now like parchment
no lemon juice can't stay.

Nothing can't erase the damage done
that dam-blasted sun nor all them black bodies
in the shadow of her grand-father's gun
where them fields was   now turn apartment block
both side the street bangalang day and night
on decent people trying to sleep.

Mrs Rosario twistin and turnin
waiting for the fight 'upstairs' to cease –
that constant commotion between sun and rain

flushing out every crapaud every cockroach
from he hiding place.

She turn her face to the wall, watch the lizard
always same-face, shaking off both sun and rain
in he one-foot t'other foot stance
in he same-way don't-care
reptilian kiss-me-ass way
while she one still here fretting
about oceans and rivers and rain
and wondering if the whole blasted world ain't the same damn
place.

The Last Kiss

Through the gospel air
a wave of blood-warm hands
ushering us forward
the word *dead* hammering in our cotton bones
our heads day-lilies beneath the break-sweat
under-arm of strangers.

Death dropped in like sudden rain.
Overnight our house had trembled
under the deluge of hymns
and rum-soaked voices
raucous as morning parrots.

Now we force our feet awake
over floorboards of polish and petals
splashes of liquor and rice.

"You must kiss you Daddy goodbye,
is the last time you gon see him."

The lip of the coffin bites into my belly.
He lies on a bed of lilies and ice
his leathered skin a map of lines
to trace in.
And now we must place the *o* of our mouths
on his cold cold skin
when, only yesterday
he looked back at me on the doorstep
sunlight crinkling
the corners of his dancing eyes.

Water Baby

When water-baby born she didn't cry
resistant to birth she fight all the way
head tucked under her mother ribs
toes curled up against the birth canal
kicking away the Portuguese explorer
who had make their land a country.
She know nothing about The Age of Aquarius.
My Grandaddy was a slave, my Grandaddy

was a slave, she singing
as he turn her and twist her till she slide
to face him and he slap her till the sound break
like a wave over the cotton sheets.

Words didn't come till later
not till she find notebook and pen and sit
in the sun rhyming *calypso* with *torpedo*
the pages of war comics blowing in the breeze.
And there wilfulness born, wildness
in her blood they say, born foot first
in water sign. The river encircle her
like cowboys, the forest sighing audibly
beneath Raleigh footprint emboss in black
rubber tread of tyres. Swimming happen later.
First she learn to fly, to learn
water baby have nothing to do with water. But air.

When Cookie Sings

When Cookie sings the world stands still
the sunray pauses on the sill, the dog
stretched out along the step uncurls a sleepy eye.
The radio dulls its News report, somewhere
a Bay of Pigs, a vote. My mother, at the cooler
stirs the coffee slow, the scrape of spoon
on tin becoming liquid, losing its' velocity
in steam, a turbulence of spin.
When Cookie sings, any children
whimpering will stop mid-howl, their ears bewitched
her singing halt the flow of tears.
Pretty little butterfly
she sings, and we forget her gums
her watery eyes, her temper weighted
with the privilege of years. *Pretty little butterfly*
what you do all day? Flying in the garden
nothing do but play. Nothing do but play
me darling, nothing do but play
fly butterfly, fly butterfly, take yourself away.

When I am grown, migrated, gone
to tune-filled lands and populous discordant rhythms
my mind over-populated with the science
of climate change and Red Admirals
there she comes, an old black woman
singing in a rocking chair
pretty little butterfly
I never knew her name.

Caribbean Hometown Blues

Now we've crossed the river, I'm riding into town
a tourist in a yellow taxi going back home.
Where once you paid the boatman
now you pay a toll
where the ferry bore you lightly
the new bridge is a stranger, clinical and cold.
So many years have passed, my heart has ushered in the blues
to play a hometown symphony, summon up the tunes.
And time is a passenger in my bones, constantly humming
the qu'est-ce-qu'il-dit of the kiskadee, Caribbean home- town
blues.

That boldface noisy kiskadee
breaks dawn in this old town
rivalling calypsos, reggae, gospel songs

he couldn't cross the river, he couldn't cross the sea
he couldn't cross that ocean
where my loved ones are waiting
worrying, for me.

But if home is where the heart is, why the blues?

Crossing the river I heard the kiskadee
reminding me of carefree times
my girlfriends and me, on our Raleigh bicycles
heads hot beneath the sun
the women in the marketplace
the smell of spice and rum.

But now only ghosts remain, these faces that I see

do not recognise me, no-one knows my name
my taxi's driving slowly through the rain.
We cruise past sparkling towers of concrete and steel
                    the wooden houses skeletal
                blank spaces where windows had been
yards dry of grass
    the hospital, the library, all gone.

And time is a donkey-cart rolling
slowly down the street
time is a Raleigh bicycle
front wheel spinning
time is a rain-filled evening
where a lover comes to town
filling her heart with kisses, sharp mosquito stings.

Where are the timbers of my father's house? Tell me Kiskadee;
tell me Carrion Crow, tell me Manatee.

'Home is where the heart is.' Nonsense. Home?
Tell that to the jaguars, tell that to the crows.
Tell that to the turtles, tell that to the otters.
Time is a toll-bridge of lies, there's no ear for a tune.
A bitter song in a haunted throat that no-one wants to sing,
Time is a traitor, a masquerade man, time is a riverman's blues
 a Caribbean hometown blues.

And I cross the river from this place once home
where the boats lie idle, remembering a time
when Charon was the boatman and you paid him for the lime
back across the ocean
where my loved ones send me blessings from their mobile
phones

They say Home is where the heart is, well tell that to the birds.
Tell that to the kiskadees, tell that to the crows.
Tell them the kiskadee girl is
coming home.

Fairytales for the Colonials

Door to door he came
down the Dutch-laid streets
suit and tie like a Mormon
shine shoes over the wood-worn
bridges, trench-water running slow.
Up the front steps, hat off
fanning himself on the porch.
The books lay breathing in his case
jumped out, spread themselves
all over the mahogany floor.

With the tamarind tree scratching at the window
and our little heads like vines
pictures jumped out of the storybooks
Sleeping Beauty and her just-dead face
jungle creeping through the castle
Snow White, red apple on her stone
-white throat and Rumpelstiltskin,
 ugly, wart-faced, spinning
straw to gold.

They stayed in our minds like shadows
wrestling on the walls
emerging at night like bats
slashing the mosquito netting.

Everyone beautiful was white
pure as mythical snow
straight blonde hair like Rapunzel
eyes as blue as cold.

No story 'bout the dougla child, the coolie
child, the flat-nose child
the hag, the crone, the witch, the drone
malformed, bewitched, dark and old

so we looked ourselves in the mirror
and stayed out of the sun.
And waited for Time to come and
paint our stories brown.

Red Shoes

Dance was in the bones like blood and sacraments like
holy water and sun, like prayers and ovaltine, like
swinging your feet in the church pews, like
dust on the streets at Masquerade, like
the gallery where the radio flung himself like
a madman through the windows. Dance was
bare feet on the burning road, the rotate of the hips
the undulation of your tits frantic with calypso. Dance and Book
were soulmates in a world with no Snow Queen no Pied Piper
only mosquitoes and jiggers, bigfoot and goady.
But come the night the red shoes waited at the foot of the bed
and everyone come swanning in, from
princes and coachmen to frogs and fish
and Carmen Miranda and the broken feet
of a mermaid sole up in a petri dish.

For Derek Walcott

When they said that nothing was created in the Caribbean
you stood up and counted us, one by one
and here we are now, shoals of minnows, flocks of swifts
skydivers, procrastinators
carving our flights across the seas and sky.
Our voices are singing across the world, our art stretch
ing the canvas from Seattle to Rome
the fastest man in the world is on the tongues
of every child and no hurricane can take away
the fact of our existence.
You came into my life late, my children needed me first
and now I thank you for more than the scratch of my pen
more than the gift of the podium to sing your words
more than my recognition of my inheritance my
blood-father blood-mother blood continents
more than understanding how you took the language and made
it ours
more than my stumble into my country's perishable beauty
like a stunned traveller just granted eyes.
If I believed in prophets there you stand on that celestial
High Altar, with the living and the dead - Marley, Smith,
Kamau, the long-memoried women -
all those who fused music with light, words like jewelled
stars igniting our names across the
fathomless
mother - black
oceans.

IRELAND

Windmill, Tacumshane

Running through the shadows of the leaning tree
Alfie
ears back to the wind
loops
a quick-as-a-whip trail
through the windmill's grass-skirt circle of light.
1836.
The last of its kind
tethered by tailpole and cartwheel
purpose now defunct
ornamental
trapping the long grass out of reach of the mower, and
offering an assault course for dogs.

He's too quick for shadows, his chase
after the ball unburdened
by the knowledge of Normans, or
the stagg
ered insignificance of
w i n d m
i l l s
s a i l s
a black
c
r
u
c
f   i   xtion
between hymn and the high   blue   sky.
Neither him nor the jackdaws nesting in the thatch
care about the Architectural Language of

caps or wings, shafts or rafters
cross-battens or shoes, only the *Now*
in the whisper
of ear
less
cornfields that used to be
and the repetitive trills of the nestlings screeching
their insatiable hunger
into the wind.

St Brigid's Well, Liscannor

If you go straight in and don't look left you'll miss the prayer on
the wall
You'll miss that you should walk round the statue five times
saying the prayer
You'll miss that you should climb the garden steps by the
gravestones five times
Then circle the cross five times before kissing it.
You'll miss the worry that you might not have any prayers left
in you
to pray at the well itself or to watch out for the sight of the eel
in the water which is a sign your trip would have been a success
if it was a cure you were after.
The not-knowing of how things are to be done
may or may not prepare you for what you'll see.
It may or may not prepare you for what you'll feel.
It may or may not relieve the pressure if it was pressure you
were coming with.
But one thing you won't miss, is the sound of all those hearts
beating.
You will not miss the hope hanging from rosaries and First
Communion cards.
You will not miss the wreaths like you see at roadsides now
fading in the cellophane. Or the photos. You won't miss the
photos –
the handsome young man with the Spanish eyes
the ordinary looking ones
the ones that still look surprised that someone was taking their
picture
or the candles half-burned or the messages piled up one on
another

RIP ... Please remember in your prayers ...Please pray for ... Gone too
soon.
And whether or not you came knowing anything at all or came
with your heart empty and your brain raised on Hegel or
Spinoza
you will nevertheless carry the burden of them all with you
when you leave, and you'll notice the notice then
pinned clear as day on the right side of the wall
and wonder if the fact that you had missed it the first time
would have made any difference
any difference at all.

The Lake Hotel, Again

This time it's raining and I am still a swift
borne in on the currents of the Atlantic stream.
This is still Lough Leane and the castle ruins
still an island in a sea of green.
A pair of mute swans are still here
on the rain-whipped waves, although the heron is not.
We are still not amongst those who can afford to stay,
but elegance and the view is ours for the price
of Guinness or coffee in the Punch Bowl Tavern.
The salmon and trout still hang on the wall
staring through glazed eyes to the lake
where a couple in black have left the terrace
to follow the spell of water. The chairs
are still upended, holding to the promise of rain
and we're all on a ship on a sea of flight
and you'll see them all if you visit at night
with their gowns and gloves and twice-shone shoes
gliding along the terrace
while the men discuss the price of war
with one more drink at the bar.
But it takes a poet to stitch them in from one century
to another, and wonder where our souls will wander
anywhere we find water.

Wild Things

In Connemara last night the cuckoo called
loud and clear like a ship's bell
a messenger bringing his business to my ear
from the thorny hedges of bracken and gorse
a whole wild cooing with the sad insistence of a child's cry
trying to make its place in the world.
And last night the midges came, a Biblical swarm of equal
insistence
swimming for skin and blood.
They had no messages but to feed and be fed
and I wished them dead under thumb and screen and spray
imprisoning myself away and beyond imagining
their millions descending on the robin's bread.
Come a morning now the mountains have drawn themselves
closer
the grass shimmering with memories of night
and the cuckoo, he's still there.

The Waterside at Cobh

The boys came in the night, piling out of the silver Mazda
with plastic cups and straws heading for the exercise machines
that in daytime resembled parking meters soldiering the space
between waterside and rail, harnessing the energy between the
fit
and the unfit who scissored their legs on the bikes
against the screams of the playground and the silent
rhythm streaming from their headdress of earphones.

Boy laughter bounced from machines to swings, cutting the
midnight peace
the soft chug of tugboats, the deep-bowelled plough of cargo
-boats accompanied by their majesty of light. Old enough to
drive, not to drink
their chatter breaking that in-between space of boys to men
boldness in the dark making them kings.

At Sea

There is no horizon, not yet
just a grey mist where the sea blends
into sky and the taste on your tongue
like stale coffee

The wind is cutting and we're keening
after the thrill of watching the land
slip away like a sigh
repair to the west in a hypnosis
of pitch and roll
enter into an engagement with an airborne
succubus – broken by the laughter of elderly Americans
heading home

I am not the captain of this ship
but my legs are sailors and they brace themselves
remembering another kind of wake
- hymns and cymbals and a blessed face
going forward into the deep
where the poet's voice cast a net
and we were catch, drawn up
our silver bodies keening
after the last host, the last ghost
believing deliverance only to come
after the last and final sleep

ELSEWHERE

On the individuation of things

That waves are not separate from the sea
or the sea from the shore or the shells crushed under your naked
feet
or their fossilised brothers cemented into the cliffs
or this passage between my palm and your return to waters
heavy in their journeying with the plastic of our generation
and the wanting whatever is in or out of season.
That the lemon too is a bastard child, an indeterminate childling
of citron, its mother-father sacredly revered, and closeted in its
perfection
from Yemen to Israel, from synagogue to supermarket
from EU label to post-Brexit. Segment by segment
they are seeking to reclaim the discovery of self.

Cross the black waters now and you will meet yourself
returning
with all those others braving the oceans.
Jonah will be there, and King Nebuchadnezzar
requesting the interpretation of his dream
and Daniel will still be explaining the city of clay
to anyone who will listen.

Four Poems from the Algarve

i. This Palm

Thirty years ago this palm was young, his crown soft and green
uncurling like a fern or the soft nub of a fawn
his stem would have been pliant, eager, firmed into the earth
by muddied fingers, quarried bricks rising out of ditches
dry with the memory of fish, growing
into whitewashed walls and balconies, angled terracotta tiles.
Now his roots raise the patio slabs, under a washing line
dancing with bikinis, his withered stubs of bark
spiralling its widened girth like a crown of thorns.

ii. Escalator, Playa de Pescadores

Young girls, the drums of their bellies taut
embrace the sun, *are* the sun
in cropped t-shirts, bikini tops
hipster shorts on bare-assed cheeks
jewelled sandals
riding the escalator down to the beach.

Portly husbands with portly wives run their eyes
of hunger. Descent and ascent coalesce
clatter against chalk cliffs
children in jelly shoes
a man with two crutches
a boy with a cardboard sign
rescue cats, their empty bowl.

The sea, in his endless assault on the sand
watches the escalator bearing them down like a chariot

to wander his fingers of foam with bare and sandalled feet
and stare dreamily at horizons they have no words for

Each tide he breaks the bones of anchored rocks,
flings himself across the sand, reaching in his wake
to haul them all in, drown them like purses
scatter them like contraband.

iii. The Strip, Albufeira

Evening.
Stuttering flashes of neon shatter the eyes
iridescent pinks and high-viz oranges
pulsating against the rhythm of techno pop, soul, hiphop
a yellow brick road, a cobbled highway of moons
broken by doorways of light, archways sentried by touts
waving cards of culinary hieroglyphics
wicker chairs, high gloss tables, football screens
replicated prisms on mirrored walls.
Fairground Bronco Billies ride on patios
dodgems spin, bronzed boys from Skegness
raise pints at girls in white lace teetering in spangled heels.
Young policemen idle by the crossroads
wild lions watching the procession of girls
and couples, kids and Granma, and the stalls
of leather and jewellery where the guys from the Ivory Coast
settle back in folding chairs, filming the night
with their blanket eyes.

iv. Slave Market, Lagos

A market on a harbour wall
not any harbour, *this one.*

Walk along the promenade now
along the sun-filled wall
even the fisherman is beautiful
leaning his bicycle against the stone.
Stalls stretch
the length of your gaze
an endless array of fake designer purses
and diaphanous scarves clutching the wind.

The locals are smoking ganja
on the cobbles   spin
on three-wheeled bikes like conquerors
in the shadow of the steeple
the cross commanding the skyline

where Henry the Navigator on his marble throne
faces the sea   slave market
at his back, just as you dreamt it
sturdy walls and ironed gates under the knuckles
of backpackers with their knotted hair
and plastic vials of coke

here are the ghosts
whose blood circumnavigates your veins
five hundred years

of that ocean
the old Fort now settled in mud, cannons
fodder for Instagram and Facebook
a schooner on the skyline   and
the monk   still staring out to sea
petrified.

Not the Season for Songbirds

when you hear about the children cupping their small hands
to capture robins, and bold men swaggering down the hills
dressed in cartridge belts of carcasses pitted with buckshot
when your mind's eye swims with the vision of Maltese trees
adorned with feathered bunting like shreds of coloured kites
filleted between the bones of budding limbs and greening bark

it's not easy to think of birdsong.

There, on that island midway between Gods
midway between worlds where spirits turned skyward
and Knights Templar rested their journeying hearts
into tombs of gold, the spirit of Ascension
rises into the cathedral of air
trapping all that flies, flits, falls   to sacrifice.

Alleluias flush blooded hearts like picks
making men of boys, taming tigers grown soft
on poolside loungers, fast food restaurants
halting passages mid-flight
small birds like prayers anointing
the blue of a Mediterranean sky

and somewhere in Sussex or Chard, some gardener
will miss a swallow, a swift, a chiff-chaff
and lend his ear to a silent, empty sky.

Sunflowers, Ukraine, July 2014

Forcing their way
through the sunflowers' upturned
faces, fields rippling with harvest.
Boots and rifles batter stalks
tear-shaped feathered leaves, black seeded
breaking hearts of summer. They fall apart, bruised thighs
and underbellies raked for body parts
passports, a black box.
This year the harvest will fail.
Who could gather and grind one grain that has borne witness
to this shower of manna so bitter the tongue will recoil
bowels erupt like these fields, forever haunted
by the silent cries of every man, woman, child
expelled from the sky, becoming seed.

WhaleSong
(After Akomfrah's *Vertigo)*

Down to the sea in ships, in ships
Down to the sea in ships
Where the clouds spin and the wind rides
Down to the sea in ships
Down to the sea with a song on your lips
Women's ribs in corsets of bone
Whalebone whalebone, from bosom to hip
Down to the sea in ships

And Johnny Boy he went to sea to sea to see to sea to see
Brave and bold a sight to behold a whaling ship
A whaling ship brave and bold on the ocean flow
A prayer for Johnny and all his mates
Songs on their lips and fingers itching shoot that harpoon
See it fly beneath the blue Atlantic sky
And there she blows the beast herself
Up from the deep, the Devil's deep
Save Us Lord! Save us! from the biting winds
The ocean's teeth, Save us Saviour! Save us!
Haul Away, Haul Away! Slice her belly
Slice it quick, with knife and pick, *Shoulders men!*
She brings the sea to wash the decks
Blood and water, froth and brine
And from her womb the babe asleep, giving her meat
To Johnny and Spike and Norm and Lars
Hacking through her heart and bone
And their very souls
Men so bold, down to the sea in ships
With harpoons, dreams, prayer and song
From London town where men of might

Their gold rings flashing in the night
Confer the price of flesh and bone
Man bone woman bone child bone whale bone
Sugar and tea all come from the sea in ships
In ships in ships, cargo ships, all come from the sea
The sea the sea the
Bloody
Beautiful
Brutal
Sea.

Snapshots

He is making his name
taking snapshots of crying children

barefoot in muddied camps
their mothers railing against thin barbed fences
intricately formed as Macedonian lace
where black-garbed women weave
their olive-stoned hearts into remembrance.

He brings them back to a soft-lipped study where he uploads
them digitally from shot to shot
noting his tar-stained fingers
fleetingly reflecting on a time when prints hung to dry
in dark rooms, stamp-sized paper-thin snapshots
of men and guns, Hemingway's time.

But now there is no handling required
no touch involved;
they're uploaded instantly onto the net
where, like stars
they circle silently
and voicelessly against the dark
mangled cloak of eternity.

The Coast of Silence

The children of the sea are sailing the coast of silence
their tongues are grooves in which to hide the mimicry of birds.
Their mother's face lies broken on the bow.

She is the Marie Celeste,
bubbles of almost speech rising through her hollow bones
the surface always shifting, a rolling ocean floor.

Love knits rough bed-fellows. Blackbeard haunts the shores.
He roams freely now, his wives are half alive, breathing
in an underworld of broken toys and shoes.

Sometimes lifeboats call, with megaphones and ropes
but the children know about monsters
who will prise them off the only craft they know
maroon them even further out to sea.

So they hold their tongues, say nothing.

Even the dog has learnt not to howl. Confined in cargo
the world is in his eyes as he watches you break through
the cloud of morning, place your hand through the bars, stroke
him.

Victoria Amazonica

and when they tore you from your roots
wresting with both hands into that lake of silence
where only the cries of birds break
the ceiling of rainclouds
showering you with more glory
than the conquistadores' swords
of silver
did sweet promises anoint the rape
of you
were you ready for such a migration
did you know
one day
entire glasshouses would be built to home you
and children dressed like Alice sit for portraits
on your lily pads
still as an Essequibo morning?

And in the unknowing would
Schomburgk
let drop his oar
or fall into a tangle of mangroves
so no-one would sing your name
Lily, Lily, Lily, Lily.

From specimens found by botanist Robert Schomburgk in British Guiana, John Lindley established the genus Victoria in 1837. The plant was presented at the Crystal Palace Exhibition, its size shown off to full advantage as children were photographed sitting on its pads.

A Tropical Depression

Tonight I dreamt my lemon, heard him singing on the
new spring tide, in oceans
where the beaked whales hide.
He seemed not to mind the weather, allowing himself
to spiral in the cyclone of rain
a buoy unanchored, fearless,
singing Leonard Cohen's *Lover Lover Lover.*

And those that heard him came: a turtle wrapped in plastic,
dolphins necklaced in fishing lines. And pith and kin from
islands,
pawpaws and limes from reefs and plantations
accompanied by a choir of coral and a pianist from New
Orleans, and above them all, at perigee, a bright
and lemon supermoon lighting up the sea.